I Do . . .
Every Day

Other Abingdon Press Books
by Cynthia Bond Hopson

Rainy Days, Mondays, and Bad Hair Days:
Wisdom and Encouragement to Lift a Woman's Spirit

Too Many Irons in the Fire
and They're All Smoking

I Do . . .
Every Day

Words of Wisdom for Newlyweds
and Not So Newlyweds

CYNTHIA BOND HOPSON
ROGER A. HOPSON

Abingdon Press
Nashville

I DO...EVERY DAY
WORDS OF WISDOM FOR NEWLYWEDS
AND NOT SO NEWLYWEDS

Copyright © 2011 by Abingdon Press

This book is printed on acid-free paper.

Library of Congress Cataloging-in-Publication Data

Hopson, Cynthia A. Bond, 1955-
   I do–every day : wisdom and encouragement for newlyweds and not so newlyweds / Cynthia Bond Hopson, Roger A. Hopson.
      p.   cm.
   ISBN 978-1-4267-1479-5 (trade pbk. : alk. paper)
   1. Marriage–Religious aspects–Christianity–Meditations.   2. Spouses–Prayers and devotions.   I. Hopson, Roger A.   II. Title.
   BV4596.M3H67 2011
   248.8'44–dc22

                                                                            2011008187

Scripture quotations are taken from the *Holy Bible,* New Living Translation, copyright © 1996. Used by permission of Tyndale House Publishers, Inc., Wheaton, Illinois 60189. All rights reserved.

11 12 13 14 15 16 17 18 19 20—10 9 8 7 6 5 4 3 2 1

I am my beloved, and he is mine...for Roger.
—Cynthia

My dream weaver, shelter, and joy. God bless
the day I found you.
—Roger

Contents

CONTENTS

A Note from Cynthia and Roger

Being married is a special gift from God. Whether today is your first day together or your 12,045th one (but who's counting?), your spouse is a big part of your life. At some point you stood before the justice of the peace, priest, preacher, or Elvis impersonator and took some pretty serious vows: "... to have and to hold from this day forward, in sickness and in health, to cherish and honor, forsaking all others." You literally promised to live and die for that dashing and radiant person who stood there beside you. But saying the words is not what makes you married; it's living them out that counts. When the words become flesh, they can add meaning, color, character, and fullness to your life!

When our son, Marcos, and his wife, Regina, were married eleven years ago, we debated what to say to help them love and cherish each other for a lifetime. What were the important lessons we had learned? What were some pitfalls we wanted them to avoid? We made a list of things and shared it with them over lunch. Then we promised to do what our in-laws had done: mind our own business! Over the years, we have wished for some similar gift of wise advice to give other newlyweds or

11

couples who were working too hard, but not on caring for each other or their marriage.

The thirty-one devotions in this book are our answer to that wish—our attempt to bless couples wherever they are and to help them treasure each other. Each devotion includes a Scripture, a few words of encouragement or advice, some things we've learned in our marriage, a brief "Honey Do List," and a prayer.

Strong individuals and marriages are at the heart and start of healthy homes and communities. The Scriptures remind us that charity begins at home and spreads abroad, but so do respect, healthy values, acceptable behavior, and lifelong role models. So when Jesus encourages husbands to love their wives as Christ loves the church, he's saying something important and memorable.

Our prayer is that the words and thoughts in this book will be a gentle but daily reminder to love and care for each other in a Christlike way. Amen.

Going to the chapel and we're gonna get married.
—J. Barry/E. Greenwich/Phil Spector

1. When we get married, we'll have a big celebration

Scripture: John 2:1-11

Cynthia

I knew Bret was an extraordinary guy when he came purposely to walk Nikki to her car that Thursday it rained. She had just gotten her hair done, and they were giggling under his umbrella, with him mostly getting wet. Two months later we celebrated their marriage and watched them kiss every time guests rang the miniature bells at their reception. Their happiness, mutual admiration, care, and respect were contagious as they began their journey together.

Their beautiful wedding reminded me of Roger's and my lawn ceremony that was supposed to be flawless but ended up anything but. First, it got started an hour and a half late because much of the wedding party got lost.

(This was way before cell phones and GPS.) Of course, by the time they arrived I was a barefooted basket case because I had long since kicked off my cute, painful bridal shoes. Our reception, which would have been fine had we started on time, took place in the dark. When it was time to leave for our honeymoon, the lights on our "new" car wouldn't work, and we had to be dropped off and picked up from one of the seediest hotels in town since all the nice rooms in town that we hadn't reserved were sold out. Whew! In spite of the wedding day from hell, I am happy to report that we not only survived but also flourished!

Several years ago, a friend and I were at a women's conference, and we decided to attend the "keeping your marriage hot and steamy" session to get some updates and pointers. The couple who led the session asked, "How many hours this week did you work on your job?" The audience threw out numbers from twenty-five to sixty but didn't see what that had to do with the topic until the couple asked, "How many hours this week did you work on your marriage?" I sat there speechless because while I considered myself a pretty good wife, I had never thought about "working" on my marriage. The couple reminded us that you have to give your best efforts to your marriage, just as you do to your job. They reminded us that weddings last a matter of minutes, but marriage is full-time. That session was an eye-opener, and one I immediately took to heart.

I'm sure Nikki and Bret would agree.

Here's What We've Learned

- Being married takes constant attention, long past the wedding day.
- Marriage takes everything described in 1 Corinthians 13 because love really is patient, kind, and not rude, does not have to have its own way, always trusts, protects, perseveres, hopes, and a million other things, such as allowing space and opportunity to grow without being smothered or thwarted.
- Liking is as important as loving each other—if you can do both, praise God! Love is the foundation; if you combine it with respect and admiration and a strategically placed umbrella on a rainy day, you'll get happily-ever-after every time!

Honey Do List

- Write down five things you love about your spouse, and leave the note in a prominent place tonight.
- Describe a fantasy rendezvous you're planning the next

time you call your spouse's personal cell phone and get voicemail.

• Count how many hours you worked on your marriage last week.

Lord, let me show your love in all my actions and deeds. Amen.

Any kindness that I can show, let me do it now...
for I shall not pass this way again.
—Henry Drummond

2. Guess who's coming to dinner

Scripture: Hebrews 13:1-6; Luke 10:25-37

Roger

I am introverted. Cynthia, on the other hand, is not; as long as she can have ample private time to recharge, she thrives on being around people and seems to gain more energy as the day goes on. Most days I really, really like people but don't care much for mobs. Huge conventions, workshops, and seminars drain me.

So we are radically different personality types, but we have one thing in common when it comes to building relationships—we both love having friends over. We enjoy entertaining, and plastic plates and cups are forbidden at our house. We set the table every day and use our best silverware and china for company, not to impress our guests (since they rarely seem to notice), but as a way of saying to each other and to them, "You are special, and we're glad to be with you on this journey called life."

When I was growing up, my parents and grandparents taught me the meaning of hospitality. My grandfather would say that when enemies sit and break bread at your table, they deserve the same hospitality shown to those we love. In Cynthia's family, her dad would often invite extra people home for dinner, usually unannounced. Her mother would shake her head, smile, perform the fish-and-loaves Bible story, and multiply what she had until everyone was too stuffed to move. Both of us were nurtured in an environment of generosity and lavish hospitality. We honor our ancestors and pay tribute to them for the values they instilled in us. I admit my children often tease Cynthia about her corny behavior. Sometimes they imagine that she sits around thinking up reasons to celebrate!

When our daughter, Angela, had her sixteenth birthday, Cynthia turned our dining room into a quaint little café and made a special luncheon for Angela and her girlfriends. Sixteen years later, Angela's friends still talk about how special it made them feel. When relatives or friends spend the night, Cynthia welcomes them with a gift bag, complete with her signature Barnum's Animal Crackers in the box with the pictures and string. When the party is over or the friends go home, we realize that our home has been blessed by good people and our lives are richer.

Here's What We've Learned

- Hospitality, graciously given, is received in the same spirit.
- If you don't like to entertain, don't. Do hospitality in a way you enjoy—call the caterer, make reservations, go to a restaurant or hotel, and get over it.
- If you don't get along with your in-laws, see entry #17 in this book. You are not obligated to have people in your home who disrespect or dislike you.
- Only do what you can afford. Don't let misunderstandings about who's paying for what cause a rift.
- When friends come to visit for longer periods of time, agree on the exit strategy *before* they arrive, so overstaying the welcome won't be part of the equation.
- Remember that your home is just that—yours. It's up to you to dictate the rules no matter how old-fashioned, whether they include no smoking, no playing loud music, or no sleeping together unless you're married.

19

Honey Do List

• Try being a guest in your own home so you can see how things work—shower, lamps, bed, alarm clock. If you can't figure it out, how can they?

Lord, let us show radical hospitality to all who enter our home, and let us treat them as you would. Amen.

You got a smile so bright, you know you coulda been a candle.
I'm holding you so tight, you know you coulda been a handle.
—Robinson/Rogers

3. You don't sweat much

Scripture: Proverbs 25:11; Song of Solomon 1

Cynthia

The joke goes this way: a mother is helping her son find the right words to say to a beautiful girl he fancies. He says the girl is prettier than a set of new snow tires. His mother tells him that the tire analogy may not work. He thinks some more and finally blurts, "You don't sweat much."

Here's a fella who needs a course in the fine art of dropping compliments if I've ever met one! But he's not the only one who could use help saying the right things. From poems, plays, and songs about beautiful eyes, silky tresses, and Ivy League clothes, sweet words make the world go round. They help us know that we've still got it and that our special someone has noticed. People who are good at giving compliments are about as common as piano-playing bobcats, and those who accept the compliments with grace are nearly as rare. (How about a simple "Thank you for noticing"?)

So what's a body to do? Work at it!

Here's What We've Learned

- Genuine compliments from spouses raise our self-esteem. Certainly it matters what others think, but we really want to impress that special person.
- There is a big difference between compliments and back-handed remarks: "Woman, if you wear that dress tonight, we may not get to the dance on time if at all," is better than, "You'd look good in that dress, but your butt's too big."
- Try random acts of kindness (giving foot massages or shoulder rubs, or doing leftover chores) in addition to compliments, but if you want the honeymoon to last, make sure you do something every week. Show and tell—that's the name of the game.
- Look for things to compliment. If the meal is lousy, offer appreciation for the fellowship.
- Brag on your spouse; it builds confidence. We work to live into our spouse's expectations and never want to disappoint.

• Try singing! When Roger sings to me "You Are My Sunshine," I hear his most genuine self. He reminds me that I'm the only woman who never laughed at his singing! No, he's not Barry White, but when he sings to me, nothing else matters—he's my first, my last, my everything.

Honey Do List

• Practice your wolf whistle. (On me, not her!)
• Practice saying "Thank you for noticing" in response to a compliment. Use it next time one comes.
• Try at least one random act of kindness this week.

Lord, help us offer kind words, encouragement, and praise as testament to you and this awesome person you created. Amen.

You put me on a natural high, and I can fly. I can fly.
—Merle Haggard

4. I believe in you; you believe in me too

Scripture: 1 Thessalonians 5:9-12, 15-18

Roger

Soon after we were married, I developed a serious addiction to yard sales. Every Saturday morning, armed with a stainless steel flashlight and Energizer batteries, I would jump into my car before the sun came up, hoping to grab the find of the century. One morning I approached a house that had a yard full of people looking up into a beautiful old oak tree with a small unidentified object wedged into it. A little girl was screaming at the top of her lungs as she tried to explain that the "object" was Arnold, her favorite doll, which had fallen victim to her mischievous little brother's antics. She kept asking, "Is Arnold still alive? Is he breathing?"

After another few frantic minutes, a yard-sale patron

climbed the tree and rescued Arnold. She laid him on the ground and immediately began to gently blow into Arnold's mouth. When asked what she was doing, she said, "I'm giving him mouth-to-mouth rededication!"

I've learned that marriage partners sometimes have to give each other mouth-to-mouth rededication because the world can literally suck the life out of you and your marriage. There are far too many schemers and wolves in sheep's clothing, and too often we find ourselves as blood-stained steps leading to someone else's glory. We can find ourselves tainted by envy, jealousy, and greed because we have lingered too long in the wrong places. We may have had pure intentions but have gone along to get along and have lost our way.

In the movie *The Way We Were,* Robert Redford says to Barbra Streisand, "You expect too much from me." She shocks him when she says, "Oh, but look what I've got!" She reminds him that she knows who he is and what he is capable of. Cynthia came home in tears one difficult day during her doctoral studies and sobbed, "They're taking the heart out of my work." I held her until she was quiet and gently reminded her that "they" (the doctoral committee) couldn't take her "heart" unless she gave it to them. "They don't know who you are or that you come from a long line of warrior women. You are standing on the shoulders of giants, and I believe in you," I whispered.

At the points in my journey when I didn't know who was on my side, Cynthia has been there—encouraging, supporting, pushing, believing, helping me find a new stride. It's what we do. Oh, and I went ahead and ordered my new graduation suit!

Here's What We've Learned
- There's always a conehead somewhere to put up road-blocks—keep stepping.
- Be your spouse's biggest cheerleader, and she will soar!
- Believe in God, yourself, and others. The rest is easy.

Honey Do List
- Dream big dreams for your future, and set goals this weekend to make them happen.

Lord, with you we know that anything and all things are possible. We claim and believe that you have plans for us—plans to nurture us and give us a future. Direct our paths to the right people, places, and things to help make our dreams come true. Help us be patient, prepared, and purposeful. Amen.

Yesterday's gone, sweet Jesus.
—Marijohn Willkin

5. Whose bed have your boots been under?

Scripture: Psalms 51:7-17; 103:1-12

Cynthia

"I haven't been good, and I'm not that good right now."

That's how the song begins, and it goes on to talk about Jesus, who is good all the time. I don't know that I'd have put the first part quite that boldly, but most of us have skeletons in our past that are just waiting around to rattle. Maybe your past is pure and uneventful, or it may be a little more colorful than you would care to discuss with your mother, but the wonderful thing about the past is just that—it is in the past. There's nothing you can change about it, and while I try not to live with regret, certainly there are times I'd like to erase the board and begin again.

Over the years, I have realized that if Roger discovers

anything more about me, I'll have to banish him to a remote place with no cell phone or GPS. I didn't start out telling him my whole history; it simply unfolded over time. For instance, at a class reunion I had to introduce my high school sweetheart, David, after somebody else pointed him out. Another time, when Roger was about to be appointed to a new church, I had to explain why, of all the places on the earth we might go, that was my least favorite. And so on and so on. The next thing I knew, all my business had been shared and synthesized.

And you know what I discovered? I was none the worse for wear.

Here's What We've Learned

- With anything you're disclosing from your past, please include context and explanation so that ten years down the road, some misspoken word doesn't send your marriage into a tailspin.
- There are some things that you and Jesus should keep to yourselves. Seek discernment.
- Although your spouse won't want to make comparisons, it may be impossible not to.
- Your past is just that—yours—and you don't have to make apologies, excuses, or explanations unless and until you want to.

• Childhood scars are real, and if there's something or someone there that you need to face, do it today so you can live triumphantly. Forgive and seek professional help to work past the demons. Molestation, abuse, brushes with the law—if there's a public record, share it with your spouse. Don't let it be learned from the Internet that you were a spy in your other life or that you're wanted for murder under an assumed name in Arizona. Pretend you're running for public office and come clean about the cookies in first grade and the Popsicle scam you and your cousin Lillie ran in fourth grade.

Honey Do List
• Understand, celebrate, and appreciate all you have overcome and become.
• Plan your funeral. Write your obituary so you can include all the things you're proudest of. No, nobody's getting up a load to Gloryland in the morning, but preparation for this triumphant event should not be left to those who will be stressed, grief-stricken, and swamped.

Lord, create in us a clean heart and a right spirit. Forgive us for our transgressions, and let us move forward with hope and gratitude. Amen.

*We may not have a cent to pay the rent,
but we're gonna make it!*
—Steve Davis

6. Honey, I bought us a boat!
7. And a new truck!

*Scripture: Habakkuk 3:17-19; Proverbs 23:4, 24:3-4; Matthew
6:19-21, 25-33*

Roger

When I was growing up and did something crazy or
spontaneous that ended disastrously, my grandfather
would say, "I don't believe you're in your right mind."
Over the years I would like to say that my craziness has
lessened and I'm usually in my right mind, but I do remember early in our marriage when I temporarily lost
my "right mind" at a fishing and boating show. Fishing
was my passion, and going to a boating show was like getting a preview of heaven!

I found myself in a room with the most beautiful bass
boat I had ever seen. She was so seductive, I almost
needed a chaperone! I was jolted out of my love affair by
the salesman's voice saying, "May I help you?" He looked

like an American version of Elton John, was slicker than a marble floor, and could have sold batteries to a firefly! After fifteen minutes of iron-willed bargaining, he finally threw in a life preserver. I left the boat show with plans to buy a beauty that cost more than my home. Now it was time to go home, put my foot down, and say in my manliest voice, "Woman, I have bought us a boat!" By the time I got home, my voice was down to a pitiful whisper as I tried to explain my plans to Cynthia.

I expected, "Fool, have you lost your mind?" Instead, she smiled and put dinner on the table. We ate silently, and I chewed every morsel carefully, checking to make sure there were no foreign substances added. I was sweating bullets, waiting for the storm to come.

After dinner, as Cynthia went over the unsigned purchase agreement, she quietly and gently said, "Sweetheart, I don't think we can afford this boat. It may be possible if we don't buy food, clothes, or keep the utilities on." She looked at me, and we both started laughing.

What a wife! No put-downs, no name-calling, no grandmother Griswold's skillet to the head; only laughter and a dose of reality. She helped me find my right mind and keep my dignity. What she was saying in so many words was, "We are friends and partners, and partners don't make major decisions without consulting each other.

31

Partners always bring honesty to the table, wrapped in love and respect." Then she reminded me that she loved me even if I didn't own a boat!

Cynthia

I admit that I may have brought new shoes, purses, jewelry, and all sorts of beautiful things into the house and left them hanging in the closet with the tags turned strategically toward the wall. And, yes, I may have changed the subject a time or two when their origin was about to become the topic for conversation. But when it comes to the big stuff, Roger and I usually stick with the three p's—plot, plan, purchase—before we bring anything home. Believe me, when you're married to Gadget Boy, who has never seen a three-tiered Crockpot, Fry Great-granddaddy, rifle scope, fishing reel, tackle box, pair of binoculars, or View-Master he could resist, this plan has been a good one!

One of the main reasons that marriages get in trouble is money and issues surrounding it. Combine that with unemployment, today's heavy debt loads, bad or sluggish credit, and differing values about spending, earning, saving, and giving, and the result can be a slippery slope to financial stress or disaster. What's the answer? Talk about it, and make sure the talk doesn't escalate from a few innocent questions into a full-blown argument. Whether you decide on separate or joint accounts, or some strange configuration of both, make your finances work seamlessly so both of you have the freedom and security to live in peace.

Here's What We've Learned

- It's best not to talk about money when you are tired, angry, or overdrawn! When you do talk, look at all your options, pick one together, and move on.
- When it comes to tithing and saving, it helps if everybody's on the same page.
- Start a little "cheeseburger fund" (veggie burger fund if you're vegetarian) that you keep and don't account about to anybody, so you won't be "standing 'round looking stupid," as my dad always put it, when you don't even have enough for a sandwich and a soda.
- Save now for retirement and the long term, but don't put off everything until then.
- If there is a disparity between your salaries, figure out early how to deal with it. Don't let it be a stumbling block or point of contention.

Honey Do List

- Discuss where your important papers are kept—deeds, car titles, insurance policies, and so on.

- Make a will for living and dying. Check your life insurance policies and the beneficiaries.
- Live like you were dying, and don't miss a thing!

Lord, help us use our resources to give, share, save, and spend in a way that pleases you. Amen.

You can't handle the truth!
—*Colonel Nathan Jessep,* A Few Good Men

8. Honesty really is the best policy, isn't it?

Scripture: Psalms 101:1-7; 119:1-8

Roger

In the movie *Why Did I Get Married?* a young, overweight wife lets her friend talk her into buying a sexy nightgown. When the woman's husband sees her wearing it, he stares and asks what the heck she's doing. Humiliated, she crawls into bed, her self-esteem shattered. There's no doubt her husband is an insensitive jerk and should be called out at high noon. You could say he's just being honest, but in human relations, is it all right to be honest when it's also cruel?

Yes, we need to tell the truth. We need to be honest, but when our honesty is brutal and thoughtless, we damage those we are in relationship with. A pastor friend of mine has to endure his spouse's constant criticism after every sermon. She compares him with her father, who was considered by many to be an excellent preacher. It is rare that she says anything good about her husband's sermons. She says, "Honey, you want me to be honest, don't you?" He longs for constructive criticism that encourages and aids him in being a better preacher. And he certainly doesn't want to be compared with "Daddy."

Married partners ought to be best friends, and best friends consider each other's feelings. This takes effort and practice, and every now and then, even couples with excellent marriages will drift into Stupidville.

A friend of mine, who usually could win a Husband of the Year award, was looking through an old photo album and said to his wife, "You really looked good back then." She looked like she had been slapped, though he never missed a beat or realized his mistake. When I saw him later that week, I pointed out what he had done. He said his wife had already mentioned it. She had let him know he'd hurt her feelings and had told him she knew it was not intentional. He had promised to be more thoughtful.

There is a couple who cared enough to be truly honest with each other.

Here's What We've Learned

- When couples care enough to be honest, they can seek professional help that might strengthen or even save their marriage. It's not cruel to say, "I think we're growing apart," or "I feel that I'm losing you."
- It's also not cruel to say you believe your spouse is spending too much, drinking too much, or staying out too late. You are expressing concern, saying that if these issues aren't resolved, they could destroy what you have worked for and, more important, your relationship.
- Honesty is the best policy, but sensitivity runs a pretty close second.

Honey Do List

- Try recording your conversations with your spouse and friends, and see whether in your efforts to be "honest," you could be more helpful by toning things down.
- Set a goal not to criticize or be brutally honest all week. See how it makes you feel and how your restraint affects your partner.

Lord, as we speak truth in love, remind us to be gentle and sensitive too. Guard our tongues so they uplift and encourage as well as constructively criticize. Amen.

I'm sorry, so sorry, please accept my apology.
—Dub Albritton/Ronnie Self

9. Don't be cruel

Scripture: Ephesians 4:26-27, 29-32; Psalm 145:18; Proverbs 11:17

Cynthia

Sometimes it's hard to count to 110 before you say what's on your mind.

Even if you like to argue for the sport of it, and Roger swears that I do, sometimes it really isn't so important to be right or to have the last word. (But, Lordy, it sure feels good when you can!) If you're wrong, say so, and apologize only if you mean it with your heart and soul. Half-hearted apologies are like that container in the refrigerator with fuzz growing in it—it may have been mashed potatoes last week, but this week don't touch it!

Love may mean never having to say you're sorry if you're in the movie *Love Story*, but here in the real world, there are missteps, mishaps, misunderstandings, mistakes—heck, an apology is always a good place to start and finish. Many couples are too proud to ask for forgiveness, say they were wrong, or request a second chance, though they may be miserable and dying inside. Then, when the apology finally comes, the stored-up anger, hurt, humiliation, and resentment allow genuine words to fall on deaf ears, and there is no healing.

I heard a story about a couple trying to recover from infidelity. The husband had had an affair more than twenty years before, and although his wife said she forgave him, she was suspicious whenever he was late or traveled on business. He assured her that he wanted to mend their fragile relationship, but she couldn't help bringing it up and wallowing in the hurt, so it was hard for their relationship to heal. To her, his "I'm sorry" and "Please forgive me" seemed empty, even though he was contrite, repentant, and working full-time to regain her trust.

I have likened broken trust to a broken cup—even if you put the big pieces back together, there are always missing fragments that keep it from being good as new. And though it may look like it did earlier, it's never as strong.

Here's What We've Learned

• Prayer makes the difference. Pray without ceasing, just like the Bible says!

- Being right is *not* the only or the most important thing.
- Talking is fine, but listening is better. And when you're listening, make sure you hear what *isn't* being said. (This is not the same as mind reading!)
- Don't get caught up in history. Stick to the situation at hand, and avoid declaring, "You always say" and "You always do." Forget the word *always*! Start with an *I* statement and go from there.
- Resolve your differences before you leave the house or go to bed.
- Say only what you would want said back to you. Think twice before you speak—harsh words are hard to retrieve. If you let civility take a backseat, it is indeed a slippery slope. Kindness begets kindness.
- You have the power to make your home a place of peace instead of a war zone. Call a truce and agree to disagree.
- Trust is difficult to rebuild—keep it at all costs.

Honey Do List
- Listen without interrupting, even though you think you know what's coming next.
- Don't be afraid to pick up the phone and say I'm sorry.
- If you smell an argument brewing, call a half-day truce to gather your thoughts and identify what the real issue is.

- Watch *Sex and the City 2* together, and see what happens when anger and hurt reign instead of love and forgiveness.

Lord, I know that kindness is a salve. Please let me apply it liberally and often. Amen.

I got it bad, and that ain't good.
—Paul Francis Webster

10. I know you're tired, because you've been running through my mind all day

Scripture: Song of Solomon 4

Roger

Aunt Velma was a special lady, and about a year before her death at age eighty-seven, she came for Christmas dinner sporting red leather pants, a matching fur jacket, and a seventy-seven-year-old man she sweetly called Baby. When I teased her, she said, "You're never too old to court, and too many of you married folks stop courting at the wedding chapel!" Her words still haunt me years after her death because I have seen many couples who have stopped courting and have settled for what I term *maintenance marriages*. By my definition, in a maintenance marriage partners do just what they're supposed to do and nothing more. Flowers are never sent except on birthdays and anniversaries, if then, and never "just because it was Monday and you were running through my mind."

Maintenance marriages never deviate from the script, so life becomes a series of pot roast Thursdays, fried chicken Sundays, and get lucky Tuesdays. Before you know it, life is so predictable and boring that you drown in a sea of sameness. Bored couples are like wounded fish in a shark tank and become easy prey for worldly temptation.

One of my friends was given a very expensive set of golf clubs as a bonus from his company. An avid golfer, he was overdue for a nice set of clubs. One of his friends owned a limousine service and also was a serious golfer. My friend swapped his new clubs for some limo time, packed a picnic lunch, surprised his wife at work, and gave her a magic carpet ride. Obviously, my friend understood the need for ongoing courtship.

No matter what kind of day I'm having, it improves when Cynthia calls and says, "Hi, cute guy!" or when she whispers something that makes me blush. The concert tickets, intimate getaways, special dinners, and mystery trips all say, to borrow a line from Willie Nelson's classic, "You were always on my mind."

Here's What We've Learned

- We all crave order in our lives, but there is a thin line between order and rigidity.
- We should treat each day as a special gift from God and as a blessing and unique opportunity to express appreciation for our soul mates.
- Intimate calls, flowers, love letters, special dinners, Post-it notes tucked inside the travel kit, words of encouragement—all remind our spouses we're not taking them for granted.
- Hearing "I love you" never gets old. Showing it is even better.

Honey Do List

- Rent the movie *Date Night* and watch it with your spouse.
- Start a date fund with your spare change. Toss it all in for a year, and use it for a special dinner or event.
- Send some flowers to your honey today, along with a coded message for which you have the only decoder ring!
- Put on your high-heel sneakers and go out tonight!
- Read *The Five Love Languages* by Gary Chapman. You'll learn a lot!

God, help me make an extra effort to keep the fire kindled in my marriage. Remind me to say sweet things and never, ever get too old to court! Amen.

Seeing that black dress hit the floor,
All I can think about is gettin' you home.
—Batten/Blazy/Young

11. Behind closed doors

Scripture: 1 Corinthians 7:3-6; Hebrews 13:4

Cynthia

In one of my favorite comic strips *Arlo and Janis,* Janis
is getting dressed one evening, and from the other room
Arlo calls, "I hear you in there putting on that black underwear!" I love it! The special rhythm and understanding that couples develop over time are the stuff that love
songs are made of. Lovemaking is a special part of being
married, and it is as different from "having sex" as the
east is from the west. At the heart of lovemaking are ten-
derness, intimacy, mutual respect, sensitivity, patience,
and a lifetime of good conversations.

I am convinced that the quality of the lovemaking is
directly related to the quality of communication and

intimacy that couples share outside their bedroom. Sustained relationships are built on much more than what goes on in bed, and what turns your crank must be sensitively discussed if this critical part of your marriage is going to work. Sex is a powerful weapon and should never be used for punishment or reward. Busyness, stress at work, stress in the family, expectations, depression, childbearing challenges, health issues other than the "headache"—so many things can put your love life on the back burner if you're not careful. And even when you are careful, it's difficult to get in the mood if the argument from this morning is left to simmer all day. Of course, if you're fighting just so you can make up, don't mind me!

Here's What We've Learned

- There may be sexy and flannel, but we sure haven't found it.
- It's all right to say what you like and don't like.
- Being sexy is a state of mind and body; they work in harmony.
- Quality is as important as quantity.
- Intimacy is sometimes holding, cuddling, you fill in the blank!

- There is nothing sexy about watching somebody brush his or her teeth or floss, so please do it privately.
- Counselors are our friends and can help get us past relationship hurdles and "issues" from our past.
- Paying attention to your body may add years to your life and marriage. Get regular checkups. Remember that pain is information and information is power.

Honey Do List
- Make sure sexy underwear is the rule rather than the exception.
- If your romantic intervals have become "catch as catch can" rather than a special part of your marriage, remember that you always make time for what you want to do. If you're not making time for this, why not?
- Start an exercise program so the muffin top and love handles are in the kitchen and the six-packs are where they belong!
- Plan an electronics-free rendezvous weekend, complete with massages, passion-generating music, chocolate-covered strawberries, rose petals, and long walks. Oh, and take that fragrance that does the trick every time—yes, that one. Act like teenagers, but not in the backseat of the Chevy; there are laws against that, and you don't want to visit the chiropractor!

Lord, thank you for this special part of our marriage—
it brings us closer to you and to each other.
Keep us faithful and keep our marriage
bed undefiled so that we may live in
peace and harmony with you. Amen.

Don't make me over, now that you know how I adore you.
—*Burt Bacharach*

12. Don't make me over

Scripture: Genesis 1:26-31; 2:18-25

Roger

I must admit that I'm plumper than the average bear, but I'm working on it. Over the years there have been too many Krispy Kreme donuts and not enough fruits and veggies. Unfortunately the airlines have designed the seats for Barbie and Ken and forgotten all about us Cabbage Patch Kids! I try to use airlines that have open seating, since fat guys stay away from other fat guys and all is right with the world! And my daughter told me that when I frown, I look menacing and people avoid me.

On one flight I had gotten my seat and had the whole row to myself. I rejoiced until a little freckle-faced, blue-eyed boy got on as the door was closing. The flight attendant said, "Young man, where would you like to sit?"

He looked around the plane, pointed to me, and said, "With him." There was a seat between us, so I figured all was not lost.

After he sat down, he asked, "What you reading?" It was one of John Grisham's novels, and I told him so. The young man replied, "He's cool, but he ain't no William Faulkner, is he?" I thought, *Lord, what have I gotten myself into?* He opened his bag and brought out a single Twinkie and broke it in two. Taking a bite out of the biggest piece to make it even, he handed it to me. I declined. Amazed, he said, "A guy your size is always hungry!" Okay, I ate the Twinkie. Then he brought out a bottle of something green, drank half, and handed it to me. Twinkie dregs floated on top. I closed my eyes and gulped it down, crumbs and all. He said, before dozing off, "I'm going to see my grandparents. I love my mama and daddy, but they're always trying to fix each other. My grandparents are old—they don't need no fixing!"

His words haunt me still as I think about the promises Cynthia and I made. We would push but never drag each other where we didn't want to go. We would talk to, encourage, hold, and hold each other accountable, but no fixing.

Trying to fix our mates signals that their opinions are

less important than ours. It says I know best. It says I need you to wear your hair a certain way, regardless of how you feel. It says this works for me even if it doesn't work for you.

I visited one of my colleagues in ministry and was greeted by his wife, who was dressed like June Cleaver. He was formally attired as well, and as she brought in coffee and cinnamon rolls on a fancy tray, I asked if they were on their way out. He said no, they dressed like that at home in case some of their parishioners dropped by. "My wife wants to come home from work and get casual," he told me, "but I keep reminding her, she's a pastor's wife and needs to be ready in case we have to go out in a hurry." The fatigue in her eyes said he had made her into somebody she barely recognized, and she had participated by going along to get along.

Here's What We've Learned

- Each person needs to be free to express his or her individuality and pursue dreams and goals, as long as they don't dishonor God.
- The only person you can change is yourself. Learn to see your spouse's good traits, and look past the annoying ones.

51

Honey Do List

- Make lists of the things that most annoy you about each other, then exchange lists. It'll be pretty clear that nobody's perfect!
- Make lists of the things that you most appreciate about each other, then exchange lists. Celebrate who you are and who God has created you to be. Oh, and pass the Twinkies!

Lord, help me be my best self and keep my "funny ways" to a minimum so we can live in peace. Amen.

...to have and to hold from this day forward...
—Ritual of Christian marriage

13. If you don't know what you're doing, you'd better ask somebody

Scripture: Ecclesiastes 4:9-12; 5:4-7; Mark 10:6-9

Cynthia

If you grew up in a home where your parents were married, you kinda sorta knew what you'd gotten yourselves into and what was involved in "being married." If you didn't, maybe you based your ideas about marriage on television couples—Lucy and Ricky Ricardo, Clair and Cliff Huxtable, Carmela and Tony Soprano, Fred and Wilma Flintstone.

In either case, what does a good marriage look like? I'm no expert, but after more than thirty-five years of marriage, I know a little. I'm always suspicious of couples who say, "We never have a cross word." I suppose it's a blessing because in the early days of a marriage, most couples experience cross and other bleep-worthy words, misunderstandings, pillows and blankets and retreats to the sofa, until finally they learn which buttons to push, which mannerisms to watch for, and what the quirks are.

Roger and I have found that we're very much alike in most things but opposites when it comes to details. He's a big-picture guy, wanting to hear the problem and conclusion, the thirty-second version of the story; whereas I, as a serious newspaper person, thrive on the details, believing that if you pay attention to the little things, the big things will take care of themselves.

We almost had a falling-out when I got my first car. We had always owned a car, but this was one I had chosen and was responsible for. It was a Honda Accord, and it was gorgeous—burgundy exterior, beautiful tan interior, and a great sound system. My almost-two-hour commute to work was made easier by my perfectly organized cassette case. (Yes, this was a few years ago.) The tapes were alphabetized by artist and facing the same way for easy selection and use, but whenever Roger used the car, the tapes ended up all over the place. If he tried one and didn't like it, he'd fling it into the backseat and leave it there.

The first couple of times, I prayed for strength in the Lord, gathered and reorganized the tapes, and tried not to be what he might call "attitudinal." The third time, we had to have a lo-o-ong talk. Roger's antique lunch box collection was his pride and joy, and he could tell if I had dusted or moved it in any way. In our little chat, I likened my tapes to his lunch box collection. We decided that I wouldn't dust his lunch boxes (I was devastated!), and in exchange he would put my tapes back after listening to them, or he would listen to something that didn't have to be organized!

I learned a couple of lessons from that. One was that, when discussing things with Roger, I have about thirty-two seconds before he's off to another galaxy. The other was that if he doesn't include every detail I need, I just keep asking questions.

Here's What We've Learned
- Praying, listening, learning, sharing, and forgiving are at the heart of strong relationships. Master these (in this order) and the rest is easy.
- Sharing—space, stuff, feelings, dreams—is something couples must learn to do, but it is worth the effort. And learning to forgive makes everything possible.

Honey Do List
- Make a sacred time daily for devotion and prayer.
- Use the following gauge for crisis management when things are headed south: Will this matter in seventy

years? Is this the person I want to spend my life with? If I die right now, is this how I want to be remembered? If the answers are no, yes, and no, there's hope!

Lord, help me commit fully to the vows I've taken and "faith-fully give my marriage the best chance possible to flourish and grow. Amen.

And don't tell me what to say and don't tell me what to do,
Just let me be myself, that's all I ask of you.
—Lesley Gore

14. Who's in charge here?

Scripture: Ephesians 5:19-33

Roger

One of my favorite movies is *The Stepford Wives.* In this modern-day Shangri-la, the men bring home the bacon and the women cook it perfectly in the pan. The women never wear casual clothes, always heels and pearls. They move about gracefully, handling the most mundane chores with the passion of a high school cheerleader. The women of Stepford live to make their husbands happy and to entertain their status-minded friends. The problem, though, is that all the wives are programmed, like human robots, to be perfect.

Here in the real world, there is much debate about the woman's role in marriage. The Bible has been torn, twisted, tied, and turned upside down to prove or disprove—depending on what side of the fence you're on—whether women should mold themselves after June Cleaver, Clair Huxtable, or Roseanne. I am sure God did not create women to be mindless servants or simply to procreate, serve, and die. From biblical times to the present day, women have struggled against overwhelming odds to put their stamp on every aspect of life, and the world is much better for it.

During a pastors' ordination service I attended, the speaker urged the spouses (mostly women at the time) not to allow congregations to box them in with expectations such as "This is what the preacher's wife does." He said, "Don't be a doormat for anyone. You are partners who happen to be married to clergy."

Successful marriages, whether to clergy or others, are grounded in mutual support and respect, with nobody worried about power and control. As the old adage goes, "You may be king of your castle, but if the queen ain't happy, ain't nobody happy." It's true.

Here's What We've Learned

• All of us have different strengths in running our households and raising our children. I have never been tactful in dealing with businesspeople, so I leave that up to Cynthia. On the other hand, if you call our house on

Saturdays before ten in the morning, Cynthia's head spins completely around and fire shoots from her body.

- In financial matters related to our children, I am a complete pushover. If Cynthia doesn't do bad-cop duty, we'll both be working until we're 105!
- We complement and cochair our little corporation (our home).
- There will always be those who don't understand our brand of harmony and solidarity. Sometimes they make comparisons between us, trying to cause friction and frustration, usually under the guise of teasing. When people say Cynthia is a better speaker, I agree. She's the belle of the ball, but when the ball ends, she goes home with me!

Honey Do List
- Study scriptures about marriage to gain a better understanding of God's plan for you and your spouse.
- Continue to work together to the glory of God in every way and in every place.

Lord, we want to be faithful to your hopes and dreams for our marriage. Help us love, respect, and honor each other in all that we do. Amen.

We need to give each other space so that we may both give and receive such beautiful things as ideas, openness, dignity, joy, healing, and inclusion.
—Max De Pree

15. Don't fence me in

Scripture: Psalm 91

Cynthia

Roger loves to tell a story about how I like to shop and he doesn't. According to the story, one minute he's explaining to the kids why he's not going shopping, and an hour later he's at the mall carrying my bags. Don't believe it! First off, anybody who knows me understands that I'm a serious shopper, and unless I'm on some pretty strong drugs, there is no way I would take him or anybody else who hates to shop when I'm headed for my *zone*! Second, through trial and error we have learned that granting each other some personal space keeps everyone happy.

Roger has lots of friends who are women, and when we first met, I didn't get it! I sorta understood that men and women could be friends without being lovers, but not really. Soon I learned that people are drawn to Roger like ants to a picnic. Either I could put him in a box just for me and make both of us miserable, or I could share him with the world and we could both thrive and grow. Happily, I chose the latter and gained at least six or seven extra "sisters" whom I love and adore. Nevertheless, this personal space thing can become an issue if you let it.

Roger and I spend more time together than apart, yet he has his interests and style and I have mine. For instance, I love staying home and I never, ever get cabin fever, but give him about eighteen hours, tops, and he needs his Kroger and Walmart fix! Or while I enjoy a flea market in small doses, my dear, darling husband can go from dawn until dusk searching out antique lunch boxes in the most remote places, and he doesn't quit until he's knee deep in numbered booths!

Here's What We've Learned

- Take time for yourself, but keep things in perspective. If every Friday and Saturday you hang with your buddies and get lost in video games, then stop, look, and listen.
- Enjoy your time together, but don't become joined at the hip. If the women are all in the kitchen solving the

world's problems and you're the only fella with them, you may have a problem!

• If you're afraid to let your spouse out of your sight, you probably need more help than these devotions can provide. Call your nearest marriage counselor.

Honey Do List

• Write down your spouse's most constant complaints, then analyze them to see if they are legitimate and how they can best be addressed.

• If your spouse complains that the two of you never spend time together, listen. If nobody knows you have a spouse because you're either always alone or with your friends, that's a problem.

• If you and your spouse seem to have no common interests, develop some. It's easy to grow apart, and once the gulf is formed, building a bridge is often difficult. Many couples find themselves after forty or fifty years married to strangers, and they never saw it coming.

Lord, thank you for someone to share my life, time, and dreams with. Help us find a healthy balance of activities and interests. Amen.

But in the midst of my struggles, in my season of pain...
I never lost my praise.
—Kurt Carr

16. I'll leave this world loving you

Scripture: 1 Corinthians 13

Roger

A popular country song begins with an older man standing amidst the rubble of his tornado-ravaged home. He's surrounded by reporters who are about as sensitive as an eviction notice, and one asks, "Sir, what will you do now that you've lost everything?" He wipes his brow and says to the reporter, "This ain't nothing." He begins with a litany of losses—his wife, dad, best friend. He assures them that losing stuff is not like losing family.

While we should never minimize the loss of all we have worked for, in the grand scheme of things there are losses and then there are *losses*. We can lose stuff, pets, innocence, friendships, jobs, family, and health and still survive, though we may never be quite the same.

I never expected my ministry to be sabotaged by col-leagues who were supposed to be my friends. I would not accept it, even when the evidence was overwhelming. Gradually, though, I realized that competition laced with jealousy can invade even the clergy ranks, and the real-ization literally sucked the life out of me. Cynthia wasn't home at the time, and I didn't want to burden her. It was my ministry, after all, and I would suffer alone. As I made the decision, I heard the back door open. I got up to find Cynthia, who had heard my voice saying, "I need you." She held onto me as I dropped to my knees.

You can find people to help you, whatever the loss, yet even the most sensitive friend or well-trained professional doesn't know you as well as your spouse does. One rea-son our marriage has survived is that we understand what each of us needs to do to return to normality. Some-times it's getting away on retreat, talking it out, praying, or meditating. Whatever the loss, we thank God for the lessons we've learned and for the gift of each other.

Here's What We've Learned

• Grief is its own taskmaster and moves in its own time. Parents who have lost a child say they measure time in before-and-after increments. When you lose people you love, realize that you have lost something precious, and you will think of them every day. It will get easier, but only with time.

- Talking to your spouse about health decisions is critical. In 2005, I had major surgery but didn't have a living will. I wrote explicitly about the care I wanted, and although my family didn't want to talk about "stuff like that," I insisted.
- Let others minister to you when you can't put one foot in front of the other.
- If you become widowed, don't make hasty major decisions while you're still in shock, no matter how many casseroles the neighbor women bring by.

Honey Do List
- Seek help if you can't get going.
- Respect your grief and be patient.

Lord, some days the emptiness and sense of loss are overwhelming, but I know you're there to see me through. Please encourage and strengthen me. Amen.

I heard your mother say loving me didn't make no sense.
But when she put me down you stood up in my defense.
—*Don Davis*

17. Leave my mama out of this!

Scripture: Ephesians 4:29-32

Cynthia

I know I'm rare because my mother-in-law loves me and thinks I am special. My bonus siblings—the ones I got when I married Roger—love me too and welcomed me from day one. On the other side of the family, Roger is convinced that since he was the first in-law, my mother loves him the most. (Don't tell Roger, but she has convinced the others that they're her favorites too.) Yes, in the in-law department we've been blessed beyond measure.

One of my favorite scenes in the movie *The Family That Preys* comes as the daughter-in-law confides in her mother-in-law that the husband/son is cheating. The mother-in-law delivers her usual put-downs, then finally understands and comes to respect the daughter-in-law after realizing she is strong, smart, and determined to take matters into her own hands. The key lesson for both women is that they have someone in common they both care about, and when they work together, both can be triumphant. But, Lordy, theirs was an uneasy, difficult relationship until they came to that point.

We've had mixed feelings about some of the folks our children have brought home—the ones we call the almost-made-the-cut crew. Although there were some obvious mismatches, we tried not to interfere. (Okay, we had to be taken to the back room a couple of times about one of them, but generally we behaved.) We also learned to keep quiet about our dislikes and especially our likes because the more we liked something, the more things our children found wrong with it!

Nevertheless, being an in-law is pretty serious. After all, when you marry, you don't just get your spouse; you get the good, the bad, and the OhMyGosh! Each of us is a culmination of every lesson, habit, and event we have been exposed to—whether intentionally or just by being in the right place at the wrong time—and brothers, sisters, aunts, uncles, cousins, and in-laws ad infinitum most likely have influenced your spouse in some way. Understand that we teach as we have been taught, parent as we have been parented, and treat our spouses as we have seen spouses treated in our familiar settings, unless something pretty drastic causes us to deviate from it. If you've seen only dysfunctional relationships, that's what "normal" looks like, and you will have to work past that. And sometimes no matter what you do, your new family makes a judgment, and you are tolerated rather than valued and welcomed.

Here's What We've Learned

• When it comes to in-laws, state your opinions privately. You can say the same thing your spouse just said, but somehow it sounds harsher, less sensitive, and too intrusive coming from you. This is one of the times when blood wins out.

• Treat your new family members as you want to be treated, and share what they offer. If for some reason beyond your control they don't like you, there's nothing you can do about it. Just move on.

Honey Do List

• Do some genealogical work so you can get to know your family tree better.

• Share health information, where pertinent, and family stories.

Lord, we are blessed to have a family that cherishes, loves, and supports us—let us be those things to our family as well. Amen.

Rub my feet, gimme something to eat.
Fix me up my favorite treat...
—Lange/Twain

18. I don't know nothing about birthing no babies

Scripture: Genesis 2:20-23

Roger

I was the oldest of the ten children reared by my mother, who was a strict disciplinarian, a nurturer, and a community matriarch. She was widowed when I was sixteen, and she led me to believe that a speck of dirt would kill a whole community.

Mrs. Bernice Esterlene Goodlow Hopson fought germs like it was her mission in life, and she taught her five sons how to do chores, just as she taught her daughters. There was no such thing as women's work or men's work. There was just work. We picked up after ourselves, washed, mopped, vacuumed, and did every household chore equally. As bachelors, we Hopson men could take care of ourselves. As married men, we had spouses who knew they could trust us not to wash the whites and colors together or bathe the children in Lysol!

When Cynthia and I got married, I dreamed of having a peaceful place somewhere between television's fictional Cosby and Walton clans. But here in the real world, there are no golden scripts. Furniture will get dusty, dishes and clothes will have to be washed, meals will have to be cooked or nuked, and by George or Jane, somebody's got to do it!

I am amazed at the excuses that some spouses, especially women, accept from their mates about not helping with housework: "Well, my daddy didn't!" "Real men don't do girly work." "Outside stuff is for men, and inside stuff is for women." "It's somewhere in the Bible: Men shall not do housework." "I don't know nothing about (a) changing diapers, (b) making beds, (c) cleaning the shower, (d) turning on the oven, or (e) setting the table. And (f) I'm too tired!" Before dual careers, these flimsy excuses were bad enough, but today Helen Reddy's "I am woman, hear me roar" would probably be replaced with, "If I don't get some help, hear me growl!"

I am blessed because Cynthia and I are passionate about our life callings, and we try desperately to limit our stress. Our home, as a result, is neither a shrine to Martha Stewart nor like Macy's the day after Christmas!

Here's What We've Learned

- We work to make our home a retreat from the world, our nest. For it to be that, we determined together how it would be maintained without its becoming a burden for either of us. We decided what and when chores had to be done and who would do them (me, her, or someone else).

- There are household chores that Cynthia enjoys (no, there aren't really), but we don't have "girl" or "boy" chores.

- The key to a happy and secure nest is sensitivity. It really doesn't matter what other guys don't do; it ain't about them. They don't live at my house—I do.

Honey Do List

- Ask tough questions: Is there a Hansel-and-Gretel-like trail of crumbs leading to your chair? What more could you do to help out? Do you nag about things that won't matter a month or a year from now? Does anybody really want to eat off your floor? When was the last time you skipped the dusting and went to the movies?

Lord, let us be sensitive to the things around the house that have to be done. Help us pitch in so that the burden is lessened. Amen.

*Take six months to mind your own business
and six months to leave other folks' business alone.*
—The Williams Brothers

19. What happens in Vegas, stays in Vegas

Scripture: Philippians 1:9-11

Cynthia

The thing I love about small children is that no matter how many times you tell them not to discuss what goes on at home, as soon as the opportunity presents itself, they will tell everything. Roger swears that if you give them a soda and a cupcake, they'll cross their legs and talk until bedtime! They haven't a clue that they've told about the fight, the yelling, the screaming, the sulking, the name-calling—everything! And you know what? Sometimes, when we get together with our family and friends, we do exactly the same thing. We discuss our finances, squabbles, love life, plans, and activities. It doesn't take long for our business to be the community's business.

Don't do it!

It is not anyone's else's business how often you make love, how good it is or isn't, how many bank accounts you have and how much is in each one, how much your spouse makes, how you handle the chores—these are private matters, not conversation starters. Surely you know people who take what you say, then add, subtract, multiply, and divide it into something you hardly recognize when it comes back to you.

Learn discretion. You'll be glad you did, and so will your family.

Here's What We've Learned

- Talk only to people you trust not to spread your business to the four corners. And by all means, do not talk to people who know less about handling things than you do.
- Don't compare your spouse with your friend's. Your friend's spouse may have a public face and a private one, and things may not be all they seem.
- Don't involve the family in your squabbles; they don't want to think less of your spouse...but they will.
- All couples hit rough spots. When you hit one, call a qualified professional to help.
- Be careful who you take into your confidence. Many

couples have been sabotaged by so-called friends who know all their vulnerable spots and take advantage.

Honey Do List

- This week, refrain from venting household frustrations to family and friends.
- The next time someone asks, "Is everything all right at home?" be sure the concern is for your well-being, not juicy gossip.

Lord, help us seek wise counsel and work calmly through our problems so our home is a haven and refuge from the world. Amen.

Girl, try to remember when we didn't have no shoes,
we stuck together just me and you.
—Akines/Bellmon/Drayton/Turner/Pickett

20. Memories, like the corners of my mind

Scripture: John 21:18-19; Psalm 37:25-26

Roger

Cynthia is fanatical about a place for everything and everything in its place. The trouble is that, with my stuff, I'm not always clear about where everything goes! I do know that if you leave something in a location she is not happy with, she will find a new home for it. Because of that, with the toys, tools, and sporting goods I cherish, I make sure to put them in the places I have selected. I would hate to break a date with a prize bass because Cynthia has put my lucky rod and reel in some girly location.

Over the years, we've arrived at an uneasy truce about where things go. Of course, there are always exceptions. One time when she was in a rush, Cynthia grabbed my favorite carry-on bag to take on a flight. She didn't realize that I'd been on a road trip and had put my grandfather's special little pocketknife inside. When she got to the airport, my gracious and regal wife was caught red-handed with a two-inch, bone-handled knife and was eyed suspiciously by the security people as a possible national threat. When they discovered she was armed with a quick wit and nothing more, they confiscated the knife and let her board the flight, leaving my knife in the hands of some overjoyed security guard. When she described her ordeal to me, I admit I wasn't too sympathetic. All I could think about was some stranger fondling my little bone-handled pal and how lonely he would be without me. I thought I would never forget it, or let her forget it, either. We laugh at it today, but it's one memory we'll take with us through the pearly gates.

Some memories are the wind beneath our wings, and some scorch our tail feathers. We can't choose the ones we want to hold or the ones we want to bury. Although I probably won't forget my knife, I also won't forget Cynthia getting up at two in the morning to type my seminary papers, then getting the kids ready for school at seven and her going to class at eight. I won't forget her swollen feet after a twelve-hour shift at Shoney's, while she counted her quarter tips on the bed to add to our meager income. And I won't forget how, when the patriarch in one of our church families died suddenly while I was out of town, Cynthia bundled up the children and drove to be with the family in my stead.

I don't know where my knife is, but I sure know where my heart is.

Here's What We've Learned

- Memories really are precious. Stimulate your mind to ward off debilitating diseases such as Alzheimer's and other forms of dementia.
- Designate a place for everything so it is easy to find your things, especially your keys, glasses, and cell phone.

Honey Do List

- Ask a family member to make a video of your memories for the next generation. Describe the significant places where you have lived, and talk about the people who influenced you.
- Write stories you want to pass on while you can still remember them.
- Clean out your closets, drawers, and storage facilities. Keep only the things you dearly love.

• Start a journal of your happiest thoughts and things you don't want to forget. As you grow older, you'll be surprised how your philosophy of life will change.

Lord, we remember your sacrifice and great love for us, and we rejoice. Amen.

What we've got here is a failure to communicate.
—*Captain, from* Cool Hand Luke

21. I can't read your mind, mumble, mumble

Scripture: Proverbs 15:1-4; James 3:1-12

Cynthia

I love watching couples interact to see how they get things done.

For instance, I always loved it when we had to take my great-grandmother to the doctor in the next town because it had great barbecue restaurants, including my favorite, Craig's. My mother loved the sandwiches from Craig's, and as we drove by, she would say, "Some barbecue would be nice." My dad, on the other hand, liked to eat at home, so he'd speed up as we approached. After we passed it, she'd say, "I thought you were going to stop for barbecue." He'd say, "Well, you didn't say you wanted to stop."

Of course, my mother would not be happy, but there

was some benefit: I learned to speak clearly about what I wanted and needed and didn't expect people to read my mind... well, most of the time.

Isn't it funny that couples can clearly articulate their wants and needs to almost everyone but their spouses? Roger loves to remind me about how "moody" I am and how I can "shut down" when I am displeased about things. If you know, love, and care about me, you're supposed to realize that volunteering to do the dishes or buying "that" outfit versus "this" outfit was the desired outcome.

Most of the time, though, Roger and I are on the same page, and the few times when we're not, we have to remember that we are two people with two brains, so we must start at the beginning of the sentence, provide context, and clarify as needed. We have learned that I need and crave details, no matter how minute. He wants the thirty-second version and has very little patience with my color analysis and postgame follow-up.

Sometimes our signals to each other are misread, so what you thought you said got lost in translation because what you said and what you meant and what was heard were as far apart as the east is from the west! (Did you get all that?) Of course, sometimes what you want to say and need to say are in direct conflict with sensitive feelings and will only cause heartache. While you're thinking through a response, you might also take some time to pray and listen carefully, so you can speak with intelligence and grace and avoid frustration and anger.

Here's What We've Learned
• Say what you need. If you don't have time to cook, clean up the kitchen, and give the children a bath, say so without the attitude.

Honey Do List
• Sign up for a communication class that includes how to listen actively, say what you mean, and be more intentional in both, since what you mean is not always what is heard.
• If you can't seem to gather your thoughts coherently, write them down and read them aloud.

Lord, hear my cry and help me speak clearly so you will hear my heart and mind working together to bless you. Amen.

You're the reason my figure is gone.
—Loretta Lynn

22. I was really fine back in the day!

Scripture: 1 Corinthians 6:12-20

Roger

When I graduated from high school, I weighed about as much as the lightweight champion of the world. Four decades later, I still weigh as much as the champion, but I have added enough to include the middleweight champ too. I have spent most of my life trying to rid myself of one of them! Obesity is a deadly luxury that only a few countries can afford, yet even the affluent countries have people dying of malnutrition and starvation. While some eat to live, others live to eat, and too many preventable diseases are linked to it.

There are a zillion diets and nearly as many has-been actors, athletes, and other notable characters who swear that their diet is the one for you. For those of us who have moved from Utopia, where Ken and Barbie live, into the land of Cabbage Patch Kids, we must also deal with cruelty from those who have the tact of a fruit fly and the sensitivity of Joan Rivers. Judging by the rude comments I've heard, people must believe that if you're overweight, you must also be hard of hearing.

During a recent church supper, a colleague said, "Don't let Roger go first. He'll eat all the food!" I wanted to say, "Yes, I'm fat, but you're coyote ugly and I can lose weight!" I didn't say it; my mama taught me better. It was just one more example of how overweight people, in addition to dealing with health issues, pay a heavy emotional toll.

Cynthia is an excellent cook—she could roast tree bark and I would enjoy it—but she is also very conscientious when it comes to nutrition, so I can't blame her for the loss of my six-pack. When I am alone, I am much more likely to grab something I shouldn't or to have less willpower. My blessing, though, is that she gently reminds me that I ought to exercise more and eat better. When she travels, she usually leaves me wonderful Post-it notes encouraging me to be more thoughtful about my eating habits. Her love, care, and concern are never laced with judgment, and I know she is praying for me to win.

We want to be healthy for each other, our children, and our grandchildren, living well into our golden years without some condition we could have prevented.

Here's What We've Learned

- Good health cannot be obtained by following fad diets or taking miracle pills.
- It is not hard to educate yourself about good nutrition. Ever since fourth-grade health class we have known about the food groups and how much or how little we ought to fill up on. The problem is, the pirates of the gastric ocean know how to make us crave artery cloggers.
- Married couples can successfully navigate the maze of office snacks, tailgate parties, ball games, church suppers, and romantic dinners and still remain fit and healthy, but it takes effort and commitment.

Honey Do List

- Consult a nutritionist or read up on nutrition, so you can make better food choices.
- Exercise thirty minutes a day at least four days a week.
- Pay attention to everything you put in your mouth—no more mindless eating.

• Talk with each other about your health concerns, and develop new habits to improve your health.

Lord, remind us that our bodies are yours and we don't want to abuse them with unhealthy food and lack of exercise. We need your strength and courage so we won't succumb to poor habits and disease. Amen.

Eatin' burnt suppers the whole first year
and askin' for seconds to keep her from tearin' up...
—Wiseman/Collins

23. Family, traditions, and the good stuff

Scripture: 2 Timothy 1

Cynthia

I started that homemade coconut cake with the best intentions. It was not my fault that the layers were uneven and looked like they had been beaten with a road plow. I'm still not sure why the seven-minute frosting took twenty-one. All I know is that when Roger came home, the ugliest cake ever baked was hiding on top of the cabinet.

I admit that early in our marriage, in my effort to be frugal, I made cookies from cooked oatmeal so that it wouldn't go to waste. Yes, they tasted horrible. And no matter how hard I try, I can't forget the blackberry dumplings that I thought tasted pretty good but prompted my usually diplomatic father to say, "I don't know who made those dumplings. I just hope they won't make 'em again!" Trust me, though, the worst was that "dump" cake I baked, where you layer the ingredients and top them with cherry pie filling. Not even the dogs would eat it.

In truth, I was simply trying to establish some memorable traditions that we could pass on to the next generation. I believed and still believe that there is something important and wonderful about having homemade dishes and desserts and about sitting down at the table to have meals together. The howls from Roger, and later from the children, soon gave way to delight as we ignored the phone, turned off the television, and basked in the pleasure of eating together.

At our house, everybody ate what was prepared and put on the table, which I always set with real plates and glasses. Nobody likes to fix meals for picky eaters, and I was determined that my children would try whatever I cooked. I made them eat everything except okra, and they were required to try at least one bite of anything to know for a fact that they didn't like it.

Of course, now researchers agree there is great benefit to having at least one meal together as a family. The traditions and rituals, they say, make children feel safer and help keep them from wayward behavior. Though it took us more than thirty years of dragging around from house to house on Christmas Day—a meal at my family's house and then at his, plus the ninety-minute travel and setup time—we finally figured out what sensible couples today learn early: you won't turn into a pumpkin if you share or alternate holidays.

I can't say that anybody's life was saved because I made homemade biscuits, baked real chocolate chip cookies, and always set the table, but I swear to you that all of that helped. Please take a few minutes to discuss mealtime in your family, including holiday celebrations, religious rituals, and parties or rites of passage for the teenage years. Whatever you want to look back on or smile warmly about, plan now. As the adage goes: some events are so much fun, you have to live them more than once.

That's the good stuff!

Here's What We've Learned

- Family meals around the kitchen table are important. Try to have at least one a day there.
- Make use of the DVR and voicemail so you can eat uninterrupted.
- Try turning off the television and playing board games or reading a book.

Honey Do List

- Share your happiest childhood traditions with each other, then decide together what to keep and what to discard.
- Try to be flexible and tolerant about traditions you're unfamiliar with.
- Deal with your own family or spouse rather than try to manage the in-laws.

Lord, thank you for the gift of remembering times past and how they shaped us. Help us treasure these precious traditions and pass them on. Amen.

Remember only what you do for Christ will last.
—Raymond Rasberry

24. We did it!

Scripture: Matthew 25:14-30

Roger

I grew up on the west side of Chicago, and my best friend, Skip Kelley, was a preacher's kid. I loved going to his home because every day there was a family gathering that involved milk and cookies, and every now and then a gigantic chocolate cake. His dad would begin with a wonderful prayer, then go around the room and ask his wife, each of the seven children, and even the visitors about their latest accomplishments.

Looking back, I don't remember any earthshaking things that came up—getting a C+ on a test, finishing a race, receiving a slight increase in pay, landing a part in a play—but the family would clap and sometimes sing or shed tears of joy for what seemed to be the smallest things. What I came to realize early in life, thanks to Rev. Kelley and his family, was that each achievement belonged to the family and the community and indeed probably happened because of that incredible support. There have been times when I've wished I could travel back into Rev. Kelley's kitchen and tell him about my family and our celebrations.

Some of our celebrations have been victories over self-destructive behavior such as drug abuse, or for a relative who's out of prison and starting over again. We know that it's just as important to support those who have persevered through problems as it is to pour our love on those who are held in high esteem. Conquering depression, disease, and debt are certainly worthy of applause, and graduations matter—from doctoral degrees to kindergarten diplomas, they signify completion and triumph. Certainly the purchase of a new home, whether a double-wide with a redwood deck and polyester curtains or a dream house of six thousand square feet, is worthy of celebration. Childbirth, adoption, and marriage are life transitions that move us to a better place.

While deaths are bittersweet, no matter the age, the greatest honor that can be bestowed on anyone—greater than academic degrees, literary achievements, and sporting, theatrical, or political fame—is to say that we know our loved one is in the hands of a just and all-wise God. To borrow a line from a Boyz II Men classic, "It's so hard to say goodbye to yesterday," but the essence of our loved ones permeates our lives, and we pass their lessons on to the next generation. We can thank God for the gift of their journey among us, and we are sustained by the memories, not of a perfect life or a perfect person, but of someone who made our lives richer and fuller.

When Emma Bowles, our family's matriarch, died in December 2008, eleven days before her ninetieth birthday celebration, we held her funeral and then the party, almost as planned. We sent her off in grand fashion: we laughed about her making us eat all our food, cried at some of her selfless acts we learned about that she had never mentioned, and promised to keep her legacy of love, hope, empowerment, family, and community at the heart of all we do.

Here's What We've Learned

- If there can be laughter, any excuse for a party will do.
- If you take and share pictures, the event lives on.
- If there are those who "show up and show out" and ruin every event, wait until after it's over to tell them about it. Don't give them the power to make everyone else miserable!

Honey Do List

- Take and share pictures.
- Tell the family stories—all of them.

Lord, we shout hallelujah for our triumphs and tragedies, for we know you are there with us through it all. Amen.

I'm the only hell my mama ever raised.
—Borchers/Vickery/Kemp

25. "Go ask your mama." "See what your daddy says." Pick one!

Scripture: Ephesians 4:1-4

Cynthia

I fixed my mouth about eight years ago and said to my mother, "Thank you for taking time to raise me." I never, in three million years and my wildest dreams, thought those eight words would escape my lips. She laughed and said, "I did it because I loved you."

I always swore that if and when I had children, I'd let them do whatever they wanted. I soon discovered that if I did, they would take over our household and the rest of the free world! I thought Roger was on that same page until about four years ago when our two children mentioned all the times he had been whipping the bed instead of them. They should receive an Oscar for best performance by children because I never knew.

When it came to discipline, my mother told you once—no asking, pleading, or negotiating, and if you were smart, you would move quickly and decisively. If she said no, that ended the conversation, and it never occurred to me to ask for a second opinion. It was like Travis Tritt's country song: "Here's a quarter, call someone who cares." Not only was there nobody who had a quarter to waste; there was certainly nobody who would have considered saving me from the wrath of my mother.

Parenting can be ineffective and frustrating if you waffle between yes, no, maybe, and "If you worry me long enough, I'll change my mind." In blended families, couple that with "You're not my real parent," and the job becomes almost impossible. Whether your family is blended, just beginning, or somewhere in between, child rearing is an issue that can make or break a marriage if you're not careful. Talk about it. Agree on what to do. And pray a lot.

Here's What We've Learned
- Present a unified front; try to make decisions together and in private. Decide who's the good cop and the bad cop, and let it be known emphatically that if your kids ask for a second opinion to override an unpopular first one, something unpleasant will happen automatically.
- You are responsible for your children's moral character.

Build it with confidence. You are their parents, not their peers; that's why they have friends.

- In an age-appropriate way, answer their questions openly and honestly about birds, bees, giraffes, whatever. Don't lie; show them that truth is the road map to trust. Better they share their curiosity with you than with their peers, who have just enough information to be dangerous.

- Talk about your finances so they will better understand how households are run and can learn early to make good choices.

- Avoid making snide or negative remarks about an absent parent, and try to treat each child equally and fairly.

- Please get counseling before you let your marriage go down the drain over these issues.

Honey Do List

- Take your children to church, and plan devotional time to undergird what you're teaching.
- Keep your children's confidences so they learn to trust.

Lord, we thank and praise you for this family—our family— in all its configurations. Bless us as we sharpen our focus to see you more clearly. Amen.

Don't forget the family prayer, Jesus goin' to meet you there.
—Emma L. Jackson

26. I pray for you; you pray for me

Scripture: Ephesians 6:10-20

Roger

Our three- and four-year-old granddaughters, Morgan and Maya, are stubborn and strong-willed little girls who are best friends some days. Other days they need a U.N. mediator. When they spend the night with us, regardless of how they've treated each other all day, they bow their heads and pray together. I doubt that couples who've battled and verbally assaulted each other hold hands at the end of the day and seek God's guidance, and yet children, in their innocence, always seem to let it go. I believe that the more we pray as a couple, the more we are enabled to recapture our childlike innocence.

When I got married, I had a prayer life about like the country song: "If I die before I wake, feed Jake. He's been a good dog." I don't want to belittle a person's love for his or her pet, but I believe God is looking for a little more. My saintly father-in-law, Big John, stood six foot four, weighed about 250 pounds, and had hands that could hide the moon. He was a great man of prayer, and the day of our wedding this gentle giant hugged me and said, "Roger, you and Cynthia have to wrap yourselves up in prayer. If you do this, evil cannot dwell in your home. Remember, prayer is talking and listening to God." Big John is gone now, but his words remain stamped in my memory. Cynthia and I learned to pray together, beginning and ending our day with prayer.

When our children were young, our meals included a recap of their school day and prayers from them that made us smile. I find myself sharing prayer concerns with Cynthia that I can't share with anyone else. I don't have to be made of iron with her; we both can risk vulnerability and not worry about judgment from the other. We are in harmony with each other and the Creator.

Over the years we have been involved in prayer groups and circles, both long-term and short-term, and have grown and been blessed by our prayer partners. Thanksgiving, Christmas family gatherings, reunions—all begin with family prayers that might last a while. On Super Bowl Sunday, what began as a rite of passage for Hopson men and boys after they reached the age of seven has become a celebration of our family's legacy. We share memories and pray for our family and for other concerns. Over the years, our gathering has been infiltrated by a few women, but that's all right. We don't think God minds.

Here's What We've Learned
- We can never pray enough to solve all the world's ills and conquer the chaos, but we can give it a good shot.
- Taking our children to church as a family is important.
- There is nothing sweeter than listening to your grandchildren's prayers. Teach them to pray and why.
- Having personal and family devotional time builds strength for the journey.
- God loves praise, adoration, and thanks more than constant whining and begging. How do I know? The Bible tells me so!

Honey Do List
- Subscribe to a daily devotional guide, online or in print.
- Let your children see you pray so they develop the habit.
- Keep a journal for prayers.

Lord, thank you for treating my prayers and concerns as if they're your only ones. Remind me to trust you and trust in you for mercy and grace. Amen.

I will always love you.
—Dolly Parton

27. So help me God

Scripture: Proverbs 3:6, 9-10

Cynthia

I propose that we add the words *so help me God* to the wedding vows, with the emphasis on *help me God*!

In the movie *Not Easily Broken,* about the woes of one married couple, the minister puts three cords around the newlyweds' shoulders as a reminder that they can prosper and go far, so long as they make God the invisible third cord binding them together. Roger and I have learned to make Christ the head of the household in large and small decisions, in good and bad times, in thought and word and deed, especially with children like ours.

Our children are both alive because God kept them so—literally. One day when Marcos was about fourteen, he and his buddies Chuck and Cornell took our pickup out for a joyride. I spotted them on a nearby street and started praying, "Lord, please don't let me kill him slowly and painfully." I am happy to report that he was spared that day. God redirected my path to the church where Roger was pastor, and the women who just happened to be there regaled me with stories of similar pranks that their children had pulled.

Another time, when our children were teenagers, we left them home alone, and when Roger got back, he checked the odometer on his car. It was obvious that someone had been driving, though Marcos denied it and Angela wasn't talking. Later that week Roger's coworker said, "I didn't know Angela was old enough to drive." We didn't either! She and her cousin Alisa, who wasn't old enough either, had been driving around the McDonald's parking lot and having a ball with their newfound freedom.

Thankfully, both Marcos and Angela have become beautiful, accomplished adults, but, yes, they're blessed to be alive. And they're parents!

God is responsible for bringing and keeping us together. God has kept me from being hurtful, hasty, hateful, and headstrong. I pray daily that I will be the kind of wife described in Proverbs 31, one who blesses her husband and is praised by him and her children in the marketplace.

If I fail, I guess I can always tie myself up with that other cord!

Here's What We've Learned
- Tolerance and patience make the difference.
- I love being married to Roger. He's the greatest husband any woman could have.
- My prayer is that anyone who wants to be married will be blessed with a spouse who will honor and trust God, and will cherish and adore him or her.

Honey Do List
- Make a list of the things that make your marriage work and the things that get in the way.
- Thank God for the positives, and be honest about the negatives. Talk to each other about both.
- Listen carefully without interrupting, and commit time, effort, and resources so God can help you make your marriage the best it can be.

Lord, please help our marriage be a testimony to your goodness, kindness, and mercy. Amen.

*This successful life we're livin's got us feuding like
the Hatfields and McCoys.
—Emmons/Moman*

28. Bigger ain't always better

Scripture: Hebrews 4:11-12; 13:5-8

Roger

I saw an old acquaintance in a restaurant several years ago, and after about five minutes of polite, sterile conversation, she brought up a mutual friend's daughter, who was also her sorority sister. The daughter had finished pharmacy school and was on about her career. "Is she really dating Donnie?" said the acquaintance. "You know, he's just a blue-collar worker."

I counted to ten, thanked her for her concern, and walked away. My eyes watered as I reflected on the so-called blue-collar people who had shaped my life. Their sacrifices, love, and concern created an environment that helped me find my place in the family of God.

That old acquaintance didn't appear to be concerned

with the daughter finding love. In her world, the important things were stuff and status. For her, it was all right to be in a loveless marriage if you had the trappings for the Joneses to admire. My prayer for the beautiful and accomplished young pharmacist has always been that she would find a compatible mate, someone to love, honor, and cherish—Ivy League school or barber college, I don't really care so long as she's happy.

My first appointment out of seminary was a wonderful three-point charge. For non-Methodist folks, that means I was assigned to three small rural churches with a parsonage that was probably less than nine hundred square feet. It was a small house for the four in our family, but we have wonderful memories of our time there. Six years later I received a new, bigger appointment. The parsonage was five times larger than my first little quaint cottage. Most of the new neighbors were wonderful but busy people whom we rarely saw. One neighbor, however, seemed concerned, and he finally worked up the nerve to ask, "Well, how do you like living out here among us?" I asked him, "Is this a secret Martian colony, or are you from some other galaxy?" He left in a huff, though I knew what he meant. It was a very affluent neighborhood, and I guess I should have been overjoyed to be there.

I must admit that the house was wonderful for entertaining pastors and people of the district. There were many celebrations and lots of fond memories, but what made the house a home wasn't the expensive Lillian Russell and Cumberland Valley furniture; it was the pictures of our children playing with their friends, the smell of Cynthia's plum cake, and the sight of our dog Sugar running in the backyard.

Whoever said it was right: it doesn't matter if you win the rat race, you're still a rat. When trinkets and trappings define the success of a life—or a marriage—we are in trouble. The stuff we fill our homes with tells the world what we like and enjoy. That's fine. And some stuff helps make life easier and more enjoyable. But when the stuff becomes a mountain of excess, and polishing the silver is more important than polishing your marriage, then Houston, we have a problem.

Here's What We've Learned
- Water tastes the same in a jelly glass as it does in Waterford crystal.
- If you're unhappy, it won't matter if it's nine hundred or forty-five hundred square feet.
- The Joneses are trying to keep up with the Fords; unfortunately, the Fords are in foreclosure.

- Stuff won't fill an empty place in your heart. Only Jesus can do that.
- People's worth cannot be summed up by what they do or don't have.

Honey Do List

- Be thankful for what you have.
- Make a trip to the Salvation Army or the Goodwill store with things you haven't worn in more than two years. Someone will really appreciate it.
- To find meaning and keep things in perspective, volunteer at a food bank or homeless shelter or for an organization such as Habitat for Humanity.

Lord, help us keep our eyes on you and not on the accumulation of stuff, for in the end, if we seek you first, you will supply our needs. Amen.

Get yourself a hero.
—Denise Lasalle

29. You gotta serve somebody

Scripture: Micah 6:6-8

Cynthia

Roger swears when he saw me for the first time, I took his breath away! He and my sister, Norma, were best friends, and she introduced us. I was visiting her to interview for a job at the University of Tennessee at Martin, and the last thing I wanted was a new relationship—even with a cute guy wearing cool clothes and perhaps the ugliest pair of platform shoes I had ever seen!

All the dorms looked the same to me, so when he assured my sister he would see that I got back to her room, I believed him. As it turned out, I ended up going with him to his physical education class, where he was a lot more focused on me than on his professor. (What can I say? I was kinda cute too.)

He was studying to be a teacher, and I could tell right away that he was different. The more I got to know him, the more I liked and admired him—and the more he reminded me of my dad! Both were all heart and were hardworking, gentle, and kind. Both were committed advocates, activists, and bridge builders, and they could get things done. I wasn't surprised when he informed me a month later that he was going to marry me.

Over the years, I have watched Roger come to embody this Micah text in his daily life and ministry, and he has challenged us as a couple to do the same. When we talk about loving mercy, seeking justice, and walking humbly with God, for us it means we share what we have; work to build more bridges through mentoring, coaching, volunteering, and advocating; empower and faithfully respect others through witness and intentionality of purpose; and seek to please God through our daily efforts and time. We know what God requires, and through grace and mercy we try to treat others as God treats us.

Here's What We've Learned

- Mother Teresa was right: "We can do no great things, only small things with great love."
- When we work together, the sky really is the limit.
- There's a hero or heroine in each of us. When we ten-

derly nurture and patiently care for each other, that li'l rascal, like the Incredible Hulk, emerges every time.

- Even when you don't notice, there'll be somebody who will want to be just like you. Give them something worthy of emulation.
- Loving mercy, seeking justice, and walking humbly with God makes life worth living.

Honey Do List

- Adopt a newlywed couple—not to provide all the answers but to help them navigate the rough spots and weather the storms.
- Encourage, affirm, and nurture your spouse in little and big ways and as often as possible.
- Plan together how to make your dreams come true.

Lord, help us to be more like you, and help us to find the inner hero or heroine hidden inside us. Amen.

. . . in sickness and in health, for richer, for poorer. . .
—Ritual of Christian marriage

30. When the storms of life are raging, stand by me

Scripture: Mark 4:35-41

Roger

My friend Jack died recently. He was a mentor and father figure. (I called him Dad—my biological father died in 1966.) Before Jack died, his wife, Sara, went to the nursing home, and it broke his heart that he couldn't care for her at home. Every day—rain, sleet, or snow—Jack went to visit her. He could be grumpy and ornery and would never ask anyone for a ride, so when he got sick and couldn't drive, he walked, sometimes with the aid of a walker. When he got to the nursing home, his John Wayne demeanor went out the window. He would be so tender with her. Now when I think about the "in sickness and in health" part, I think of Jack because he took it so seriously.

I love talking with Cynthia, and we solve all the world's

problems every evening we're together. We are radically different conversationalists; I just want the facts and Cynthia has to give you every detail. Sometimes I am short with her and have very little patience. She tolerates my moodiness and my impatience and never fails to ask, "Honey, how was your day?" I want always to be tender like my friend Jack, but there are days when I should have a kindergarten teacher put me in time-out! Even on those days, Cynthia is the best of the best. Lest I give you the impression she's perfect, be real clear: the sweetness dissipates if you bother me, the babies, the grandbabies, or a child anywhere on the earth!

Yep, we both have flaws, but Ben E. King sang our signature song, "Stand by Me," and the lyrics say, "I won't be afraid as long as you stand by me." It doesn't matter what the crisis is, if I can just make it home and put my arms around my anchor, I know I'll be fine.

Several years ago I got a call from my doctor with news that should have been shared at his office, but somehow the wires got crossed. The news was life-changing and could have been life-shattering, but I tried to be calm. I called Cynthia and our children. As I expected, Angela went to pieces, and Marcos was a bit stronger, asking how I was handling it. When he found out I was all right, he was too. Cynthia was quiet and finally said, "Hon, it'll

111

be all right." She was driving to Georgia for a meeting, but I wasn't surprised when she appeared at my Nashville hotel room later that night.

That is how it is with us. We have survived my nephew's murder, the deaths of three of her parents and our grandparents, issues with our children, accidents, tornadoes, and just about everything in between. We both know the source of our strength, and we know we have each other till death do us part.

Here's What We've Learned
- God is our rock and a very present help always.
- Together there's nothing we can't face.
- For better or worse, in sickness and health, for richer or poorer—that's what we've signed up for.
- Storms will come and our hearts will be broken, but God knows everything that happens to us and is working for our good.

Honey Do List
- Write a quick note of thankfulness for your spouse.
- Send a newly married couple a card of encouragement.

Lord, our vows are sacred. Help us commit fully to them and live faithfully in your care. Amen.

If I had to do it all over again, I'd do it with you.
—Roy Clark

31. Happily ever after

Scripture: Matthew 19:4-6

Cynthia

I recently spoke at a church where one of the men kept berating his wife, and the woman next to me whispered loudly, "Whew! I couldn't be married to him. I'd smother him in his sleep with a nice feather pillow!" I almost lost my place because I was thinking the same thing—not the feather pillow part, but I did wonder how this couple had managed to stay together. The answer, I think, was pretty simple: they had learned how to live with each other, just as they'd promised when they got married. Thankfully, "happily ever after" looks different at our house.

Learning to live together and care for and about each other is all part of the art of marriage. Cherished moments such as reading between the lines (not the same thing as mind reading), interpreting the "look" (you know which one I mean), finishing each other's sentences, tasting the salt when the other one cries, lying in bed dreaming about possibilities, planning for your weekly date—all these things remind us that we literally have only just begun, as the popular wedding song reminds us.

More than thirty-five years ago I met the love of my life (trust me, I had to weed out a frog or two before my prince appeared), and we are in the process of living happily ever after. Roger is a precious gift, and I still smile whenever he comes to mind. Our prayer is that your life together, like ours, will be filled with joy, peace, prayer, love, encouragement, affirmation, and lots of laughter. These are things you can control and work toward, and they make being married fulfilling and worth the effort. We don't claim to have all the answers, but we do hope our love and lessons bless you, your marriage, and your home from this day forward.

Here's What We've Learned
- The way you treat yourself is the way you will be treated by everyone else. Give, demand, and act as if you deserve respect.
- You don't have to tolerate cheating, deceit, or lying.

- Foolishness, goofing off—whatever you want to call it—spells fun and fellowship! Life is serious enough without dwelling on gloom and doom. The tough times will come without invitation or provocation, so laugh when you can. As the Nike commercial says, just do it!
- Laughter is contagious—fill your home with it and home will always be a welcoming place.

Honey Do List
- Live happily ever after and enjoy every moment.
- Choose happiness and peace and work toward both!

Dear God, thank you for this opportunity to be in love with someone who loves and cares for me. Help us be sensitive, interested, interesting, and more like you today than we were yesterday. Amen.

Wise Words to Live By

♥ Drink water from your own well—share your love only with your wife.... Let your wife be a fountain of blessing for you. (Proverbs 5:15, 18)

♥ The man who finds a wife finds a treasure and receives favor from the LORD. (Proverbs 18:22)

♥ To keep your marriage brimming with love in the loving cup, whenever you're wrong, admit it; whenever you're right, shut up. (Ogden Nash)

♥ It is better to be faithful than famous. (Theodore Roosevelt)

♥ Happiness is the inner joy that can be sought or caught, but never taught or bought. (Anonymous)

♥ Start out like you can hold out. (Emma Jones Bowles)

♥ Stay and work things out when things get tough—ain't nothing to this leaving and going back. Either stay and be there or go and be gone. (Anonymous)

♥ Enjoy what you have; let the fool hunt for more. (Anonymous)

♥ Always part with a kiss and a kind word. (Anonymous)

♥ If you buy happiness on installment, the payments last longer than the happiness. (Barbara Ann Kipfer)

♥ God gave you two ears and one mouth so you can listen twice as much as you talk. (Jim Frank Currie)

♥ Do what matters most at the time. (Anonymous)

♥ He who forgives ends the quarrel. (Anonymous)

♥ If you want to get more of something, then give more of that thing. (Barbara Ann Kipfer)

♥ If you're looking for trouble, you can always find it. (I'm just sayin'.)

Special Thanks

"Till death do us part" may end up being seventy-five years or one month; there is no way to know. Roger and I do know that we've been sustained by having glorious role models for long, beautiful marriages. Even the short, rocky ones taught us how we didn't want to be, so we learned from them too!

As we have reflected on what makes our marriage work, we know that God blessed us with each other, and therein lies the difference. Further, as we discussed the possibility of this book, the fervor from our friends and families inspired us to see the project through.

For our wonderful children, Marcos (along with his wife, Regina) and Angela, and our four beautiful grand-children: your patience and pride in our work have been heartwarming. You are the light and joy of our lives.

For our phenomenal mothers—Bernice and Alvis Marie—and in loving memory of the late A. G. Hopson, John A. Bond Jr., Carey and Emma Bowles, and our grand-parents, Clara, John A. Sr., Isaiah, and Irene, who showed us how to live in relationship with each other and with God.

To our loyal and fabulous siblings: thank you for the love you share with us and with each other!

And for everyone who has supported us through the years, especially Cheryl and Crystal, we are grateful for your encouragement and inspiration.

We have grown as a couple while working on this book, and we hope it will bless you in every way. With thanks to God for grace and mercy,

Roger and Cynthia